Deep Cleansing

Dora Obi Chizea, M.D.

Deep Cleansing
For
Relief of Personal Pain
&
Distress

Dora Obi Chizea, M.D.

ISBN: 978-1-7335156-2-7

Disclaimer: This presentation is the author's view and theory. It is informational and for reference, and not intended to provide medical or spiritual advice or be a substitute for advice and/or care from the reader's personal physician or spiritual adviser.

Forward

When I met Dr. Chizea years ago, I realized that she was an exceptional lady and from the Colonies like me. We struck up a relationship immediately because I could see that she had a deep faith in God, as I do, but also that she received direct inspiration about what to do with her patients. It was amazing and I felt blessed at that time.

Since our friendship has continued over the years, I realized that her writing was relevant and as she was an exceptional poet, she was able to combine the two sides of her personality to enlighten her readers.

Her new book "Deep Cleansing" was started prior to the coronavirus invasion and when I called her to ask what was the best thing to do with this virus – she already had the protocol which she gave me and when I visited her at the beginning of June, the book was written and full of wisdom combined with beautiful poetry that was easy to get her message across. As the message came from The Father, thankfully, none of her patients suffered and died of corona or Covid-19.

It is an honor for me to call this gifted woman "friend" and I hope you will love her book like I did.

Phillipa Scrivens M.S., CC/SLP

Acknowledgements

If I spent every moment of my life Thanking God, it will still not be enough for the unwavering faithfulness of God in my life. This book is once again another testimony. When I started this journey of "Deep Cleansing," I had no idea where I was going but soon found the Mighty One has a love message for all who are willing to listen. How awesome! So, I say "Thank You God" for being Our God.

Also, as always, I Thank my Family and Friends for being there for me and encouraging me all the way. My Prayer is that God will continue to Bless every one of you - Amen.

This presentation on *Deep Cleansing* is particularly special, because of the Covid-19 season of 2020, that amplified our challenges as a Human Family.

Under these circumstances, it is not surprising, that I turned to my Friend and Sister Phillipa Scrivens to review and foreword this book for me.

Phillipa, I say, "Thank You" for always being there for me and May God grant you All the Special Favors you ask of Him. Amen.

Dora Obi Chizea, M.D.

**"Deep Cleansing
For Relief of Personal Pain
and Distress"
Is dedicated to All Leaders
At Every level of Humanity,
who seek the
'Common Good' of Humanity
With Goodwill to All Men**

Table of Contents

Deep Cleansing
For
Relief of Personal Pain
& Distress

Dora Obi Chizea, M.D.

Chapter 1 Personal Pain

The greatest cause of personal pain, distress and chronic illness is Self-Bondage.

Self-Bondage cos we want
To look right for the world
Appear proper for that person
Or people we wish to impress

Belong to and rhyme with the in-crowd
That special group
Exclusive of the others
We call outsiders

Self-Bondage by our Ego
The long identified
Psychological factor
Of personality

Pride - some call it,

Self-preservation, others say
But ultimately- Selfish
Making Our Self
The Center of the Universe!

But we are not
So, we suffer

Usually in silence
With
Pent up pressure building

II
Then One Day
We lash out
At someone we can blame or
bully
And get away with it
Or
Maybe we
Decide to suck it up and
Bury all the stuff so deeply
We forget what we buried and
Why

III
In time, filled up and spilling
over
With Self-Bondage
We become physically sick –
Fatigue, we complain
Tired all the time
Sleepless and restless
Then there is Headache, Belly
ache, Diarrhea, Constipation
and more
Never seems to end-
Hypertension, Chest Pain,
Sugar Diabetes
And God Forbid other
unmentionables

Chapter 2 **Self-Bondage**

Ah, the garbage-can of our self-bondage is now too full and overflowing. We cannot hide or stuff the waste anywhere any more in our physical body container. So, we look for relief!

"Yes, I did it!" I confess
Forgive me, Forgive me
Just give me relief!"
We each cry in desperation
Sometimes in time enough
For rescue
And sometimes too late for
That phase of planet Earth
But
No matter when we ask
For Help!
Deep Cleansing is the solution.

Chapter 3 *What is Deep Cleansing?*

Deep Cleansing goes beyond just washing, waxing, brushing, polishing or shining the object, in this case - our very being. It means turning every aspect of our being inside out. Looking through all nooks and crannies. Un-stuffing all pillows and Teddy Bears to inspect every foundation-stone, in this case every cell in our body- to ensure that there is nothing hidden that has not been exposed to our *conscious awareness.* [Luke 8:17]

Recall, as a child, being told by your mother or caregiver not to eat in the bedroom; to eat only in the dining room. Well maybe it was not you exactly, but you can recall something similar happening to someone you knew as a child.

Yes, Mummy said don't eat in the bedroom because ants and other insect's even rats can scent the food and come into the bedroom and cause havoc. Yes, you heard but you could not stop yourself from eating your favorite candies, especially chocolate. They seemed to taste so much better when you sneaked them into the bedroom and crunch at then as you curled up in bed. Whaooh!

Never mind you were supposed to have brushed your teeth for the night.
Then your brother or sister told on you, or your mum walked in just to put away the

laundry inside the drawers in your bedroom and found you 'Munching'!
We will not go into the consequences of that incident now.

Yes, you thought you were very smart as you quickly hide away the candy wrappings by stuffing them under your pillow or bed. You had stopped chewing and hoped that your mother did not smell anything!
*****
You had done this for many months and now the day had come. The ants had invaded - and while your mother was spraying off the ants, she found the pile of candy wrappers ...

Whew! Now you had to give account about why you disobeyed Mummy's orders

but first you must clean up the mess.
But that was only external cleaning; the Deep Cleaning will come years later.

Chapter 4 *Water: As Deep Cleanser*

The commonest tool for cleansing is *Water!*

If you do not read any other chapter in this book, please read this chapter. It is a revelation.

We look at water and use it every day and yet have no idea what *it is* in Spirit and Life Eternal.

This chapter was actually prompted by the Readings of the first Sunday of Lent 2020. It was March 1st 2020 and the first reading tells the story of how Eve, the first mother of Mankind and her husband Adam, the first father of Mankind, *fell* for the Devil's *lie, temptation* and *deceit*

"You will *not* surely die,..." [Genesis 3:4] the Devil, as Serpent told Eve after she had responded to the Serpent's first prodding question of, "Has God *indeed* said, 'You shall not eat of *every* tree of the garden'?" [Genesis 3:1]

Trick question. To which Eve, aware that God, their Creator had put her and her husband Adam as *Caretakers* and *Gardeners* of the Garden the Lord had planted "eastward in Eden..." [Genesis 2:8]

Replied; - "We (my husband and I) may eat the fruit of the trees of the garden; but of the fruit of the tree which is in the midst of the garden,

God has said, 'You shall not eat it, nor shall you touch it, lest you die.'" [Genesis 3:2-3]

Clearly, Eve understood the rules but she *allowed* herself to *listen* to the Serpent who contradicted God's instructions and went on to pile on *lies* as *melody* for Eve's listening ears!

"You will surely not die,
For God knows that in the day
You *eat* of it your eyes will be opened
And you will be *like* God,
Knowing good and evil."
[Genesis 3:4-5]

First of all, Eve was not *physically blind*. So, which 'eyes will be opened'?
*****

The first lesson is to *not* get into conversation with evil.

The Devil or Serpent has only *one agenda* – To *contradict* God's instruction for your *good life* as Human.

God's loss is the Devil's gain
The battlefield - your Mind
and Body
The trophy – your Soul

Soul with God is Joy Eternal
Soul with the Devil is Pain,
Pain and more Pain
No retrieve
Unless Help comes by Grace
and Mercy
*****

So, Eve, like every *strong headed* but *naïve* child *seduced* by the Serpent's tantalizing idea of her eyes being *'opened'* beyond what she was *'seeing'* physically, decided to take the Serpent's advice.

"So, when the woman (Eve) *saw*
That the tree was good for *food,*
That it was *pleasant* to the eyes,
And *desirable* to make *one wise*
She *took* of its fruit and *ate.*
She also gave to her husband with her,
And *he ate,*" [Genesis 3:6]

*****

Choices and Motives

The message here is about the choices we *make* and the *motive* behind our choices.

Just as we will find in the 3rd reading [Matthew 4:1-11], we can *reject*; say "No!" to the Serpent's temptations or suggestions no matter which angle he comes from.

Eve's responses were all about the *Ego* and the *Flesh.* -to satiate them:

> She saw the fruit with her
> physical eyes; 'and it was
> *pleasant* to look at.
> She noted the *good food*
> will make her physically
> satisfied
> And also make her *wise* being
> *like* God!

What? "Be like God?"

The *idea* should make one awed and shudder with 'Holy Fear!'

But once we get on *'Ego Trip'* we forget we are *dust!*
How can 'dust' be God for:
"...the Lord God formed man of the dust of the ground and

breathed into his nostril the breath of life; and man became a living being." [Genesis 2:7]

The message here is: **Don't be carried away by Ego.**

A, ha!

Now the rubber hits the road! Eve and her husband Adam have barely *'enjoyed'* their moment of *'knowledge and wisdom'* when they realized they were *'naked'*.

Naked!
Oh, naked Man is
In Body, Mind and Spirit
If from God, he away turns

Alas!
The Devil, as Serpent
No matter how sharp tongued
Can never, Naked Man, -
cover!

Now these **choices** made; - in *disobedience* and *ignorance* and in *contempt* of God's simple instruction; -by Eve and Adam, (in their Human **Ego-centrism**) triggered *consequences* beyond their *imagination.*

"Then the *eyes of both of them* were *opened*
And they *knew* that they were *naked*
And they sewed fig leaves together
And made themselves coverings" [Genesis 3:7]

The Message: Choices have consequences. We can control our choices but not the consequences. How to handle choices by direct confrontation with the Serpent is demonstrated in **Matthew 4:1-**

11 This is a good time to take a look.

*****

Choose Wisely

Because God is *Wisdom* choosing wisely means choosing from God's perspective.

How do you know you are choosing *wisely* – because God The Creator has written within each Person *What is True* and everyone *knows the Truth within himself or herself.*

It is called **Conscience**. Don't over rule your Conscience with your *Free Will* for the purpose of *Expedience* or *Ego.* The consequences of such overrule are beyond your *control* and *remedy.*

You have to read the rest of Genesis Chapter 3 to find the *Sentence* pronounced on all *Three Participants* in the violation of the *'Rule of God'* – also known as *"The Fall of Man"*

"Cursed is the ground for your sake;
In toil you shall eat of it
All the days of your life..."
[Genesis 3:17]

*****

Now that Mankind is in trouble and has been Sentenced; when will this Sentence term? Or will it ever term?

Does it end when you *die physically?*

"... For dust you are
And to dust you shall return."
[Genesis 3:19]

Unfortunately, the answer is 'No!' because, remember – "… the Lord God formed man of the dust of the ground, and *breathed into his nostril* the breath of life; and man became a living *being*." [Genesis2:7]

It is 'true' dust goes to dust and *breath of life* back to God's Nostril. But, because this breath, has been *contaminated* by the **Sin of Disobedience**, it *cannot* be *re-integrated* into a **Pure God** unless it is *purified!*

It's like if, you borrowed your Grandma's fancy Table Cloth for a party, you cannot return it to her *dirty!* You wash it after use and say, "Thank You Grandma" when you return it. That's called Good Manners.

So, don't expect God to receive back; *contaminated* and *polluted Breath* of life from you after use. Like Grandma's table Cloth **it must be washed.** *Purified and made Clean* for *re-integration* into God.

That brings us to the question of- *Who can purify this breath for us to return it honorably to whence it came?*
Answer: Only God, Our Father and Creator has the ability.
And that, is where the 3rd Reading of the day – Matthew 4:1-11 comes in:

*****

Purifying the Soul Component of Self

The good news is that after generations of Mankind paying the penalty for the

Disobedience (Sin) of Adam and Eve, God Our Father, out of Love and Pity decided to have *Mercy* on Mankind.

After all, 'these, are His Creatures, whom He designed in His Own Image and Likeness and whose expired *"breath" (Soul)* - because of its contamination, is unable to *return Home* and re-integrate into God. They have become *Wandering Souls* – with no place to rest eternally - since God is Eternal.

Because Eternal God is the only One, who *can cleanse the contaminated soul of Man,* He decided to come as Man, called Jesus Christ to do the cleansing needed to re-integrate 'Wandering Man's Soul' back to God – so that while:

'dust goes to dust'
Breath of God (Spirit) will go
back to God's Nostril.

But guess what? The Devil, again as Serpent was back at it! Again, he tried to thwart God's Good Purpose for Mankind.

"Then Jesus was led up by the Spirit Into the wilderness To be tempted by the devil."
[Matthew 4:1]

It is not my purpose to recount the three major temptations reported in Matthew 4:1-11, which you can read at your convenience. It is, however, my purpose to point out the *contrast* with what our first parents Adam and Eve did.

They said, "Yes" to the Devil while Jesus said "No" to the Devil.

In the finish the Serpent's offers and advice were rejected and Jesus ordered him (the Devil) to get away from Him!

"Away with you, Satan! For it is written 'you shall worship the Lord your God, And Him only you shall serve.'" [Matthew 4:10]

And the immediate reward was:

"Then the Devil left Him, And behold, angels came And ministered to Him." [Matthew 4:11]

Yes, this is the *model*.
Say "No" to the Devil, no matter what his proposal – because it is always designed to *contradict* God's Will for you.

Say "No" to the Devil and he will leave you alone. James puts it this way in James 4: 7-8; "… Resist the Devil and he will flee from you.

Draw near to God and he will draw near to you.

Cleanse your hands, …and purify your hearts, …"[James 4:7-8]

"…Resist the Devil and he will flee from you. Draw near to God and He will draw near to you. Cleanse your hands, … amd purify your hearts…"

Yes, always say "No" to the Devil and you will have the *Angels minister* to you.

*****

What if you already made a mistake and said "Yes" to the Devil previously?

Do not fret!

Once you recognize the error, **renounce** it and **turn** around, (repent) – to conform to God's Goodwill for you. It is written in your *Conscience.*

> "From that time, (i.e. after the
> temptation) Jesus began
> To preach and say,
> "Repent for the Kingdom of
> Heaven is at hand."
> [Matthew 4: 17]

Kingdom of Heaven where there is *goodness* and *love* for obedience instead of the curse of disobedience to God's commands.

III

Jesus overcoming these series of temptation got me thinking:- Jesus is God, but also Human like you and I. So, how do we inherit his *Perfect Obedience* and the goodness and blessings that come with it when we are *not* his *physical descendants* as we are of Adam?

The first part of the answer was easy – By Faith. Believe in Jesus Christ, that He is the Begotten Son of God.

Next Question:

Will that belief alone help our contaminated Soul (Spirit) return to God?

"No" is that answer.

So how will our Adam -inherited contaminated Soul get back to God 'from whence it came'.

Answer: By *purification:*

Through the *water of Baptism* in the Name of 'The Father, The Son and The Holy Spirit.'
So, that's what the 2nd Reading [Romans 5: 12-15] was about. It says:

"Therefore, just as through one man
Sin entered the world
And death through sin
And thus death spread to all men,
Because all sinned ..."
[Romans 5:12]

It continues in verses 18 and 19 saying:

"Therefore, as through one man's offense
Judgement came to all men,
Resulting in condemnation,
Even so through one Man's righteous act
The *free gift came* to all men,

Resulting in justification of
life.
For as one *man's
disobedience*

Many were made sinners, so
also by One Man's *obedience*
many will be made *righteous.*
[Romans 5:18-19]

So, we *inherit* Christ by being
birthed in Him through the
Cleansing of the Soul (Spirit)
with the *Water of Baptism.*

Did you get that?

Hear it is once more. *Baptism*
is essential to becoming
Spiritual Children of God
thereby making us eligible to
inherit the *Forgiveness* and re-
integration of our Spirit (Soul)
into God 'from whence it
came.'

*****

Entry Passport

If we, as wandering Human Souls, must return to God: Breath to Breath, Spirit to Spirit; Water Baptism is a *requirement*. Not optional. It's the **Passport** for entry. No Passport No Entrance.

Jesus Himself though He did not need it, to enter Heaven (His Home), was Baptized to show us the need for Baptism:

> "Then Jesus came from
> Galilee
> To John at the Jordan
> To be Baptized by him."
> [Matthew 3:13]

However, John the Baptist, *knowing* that Jesus was the *Son of God*, wanted to restrain

himself from baptizing Jesus
said:
"I need to be baptized by You
and are You coming to me?"
[Matthew 3:14]

In response, however –
"Jesus answered and said to
him
'Permit it to be so now,
For thus it is fitting for us
To fulfill all righteousness'"
[Matthew 3:15]

"Then he (John the Baptist)
allowed Him."
[Matthew 3:15]

And finally, to *confirm* that this
Baptism is the *'Will of God'*:
"When He had been baptized,
Jesus came up immediately
from the *water;*
And behold the heavens were
opened to Him,

And He saw the *Spirit of God* descending
Like a dove and alighting upon Him.

And suddenly a voice *came* from heaven, saying,
"This is My beloved Son,
In whom I am well pleased"
[Matthew 3: 16-17]

Then Jesus was led by the Spirit
Into the wilderness
To be *tempted by the Devil."*
[Matthew 4:1]

This temptation we have discussed earlier.

*****

To underscore the importance of Baptism for *union with God,* Jesus later on in His Ministry said this about baptism to Nicodemus, a Pharisee and a

ruler of the Jews, who had come to Him at *night* to learn more from Jesus:
"Jesus answered and said to him (Nicodemus)
'Most assuredly, I say to you,
Unless one is *born again* he cannot *see*
The kingdom of God.'
[John 3:3]

Nicodemus said to Him,
'How can a man be born again
When he is old? Can he enter
a second time Into his
mother's womb?'

Jesus answered, 'Most assuredly, I say to you, unless one is *Born of water and the Spirit.* He cannot enter the kingdom of God.

That which is born of the flesh
is flesh

And that which is born of the
Spirit is Spirit.'"
[John 3:3-6]

*****

This makes the point that;
Baptism with Water and Spirit
is absolutely a *requirement* for
re-unification with the Spirit of
God. Consistent with this
notion, John reports in John 3:
22 that-
"After these things
Jesus and His disciples came
into the land of Judea,
And there He remained with
them and baptized.

Now John was baptizing
In Aenon near Salim
Because there was much
water there.
And they (the disciples) came
and were baptized."
[John 3:23]

*****

The Importance of Baptism is the purpose of this Chapter which I am delighted you have read. Bravo!

As you can see:

Baptism is absolutely essential for Salvation and entry into heaven to re-integrate with God the Father, Son and Holy Spirit.
It is what commissions you and identifies you as a Child of God who has been redeemed by the Passion, Death and Resurrection of Jesus Christ!
Like it or not; Baptism is what entitles you to 'Eat this Bread and Drink this Cup.'

To consolidate these fundamentals; **"Jesus took bread, blessed and broke it, and gave it to the disciples and**

said, "Take, eat; this is My Body."
Then He took the cup, and gave thanks, and gave it to them, saying, "Drink from it, all of you. For this is My Blood of the new covenant, which is shed for many for the remission of sins…" [Matthew 26:27-29]

It is done!

Now, you can enter into *Eternal Life, totally Cleansed and Forgiven of all your sins;* to re-integrate into Christ and become *One with Christ* just as 'Christ is One with the Father.' Hip, Hip, Hip Hurrah!

The 'Wandering Soul' now has a Home to Rest in Love and Peace!

*****

Finally, as He was about to ascend into Heaven; He commissioned His followers:

"... He said to them, "Go into
all the world
And preach the gospel to
every creature.
He who *believes* and is
baptized will be saved;
But he does not believe will be
condemned,""
[Mark 16: 15-16]

The same message is reported in Matthew 28:18-20; "And Jesus came and spoke to them, saying, **"All authority has been given to me in heaven and on earth. 'Go therefore and make disciples of all the nations, *baptizing* them in the name of the Father and of the Son and of the Holy Spirit.'"**

Teaching them to observe all the things that I have commanded you; and lo, I am with you always even to the end of the age." Amen. [Matthew 28:18-20]

Bottom line: If you or your loved ones are *not baptized,* please get *Baptized* in the name of the Father, Son and Holy Spirit Amen.

*****

Wedding Garment for Banquet

Baptism is that **Wedding Garment** needed for heaven's banquet and a face to face with **God - Our Father!**
And you don't want to be *that man* who did not have a wedding garment when the King comes in to see the guests [Matthew 22:11] and hear

Him say; **"Friend, how did you come in here without a wedding garment?"** and become **speechless!**

"Then the King said to the servants,
"Bind him hand and foot, take him away,
And cast him into outer darkness;
There will be weeping and gnashing of teeth."
For many are called,
But few are chosen."
[Matthew22: 11-14]

Get your **Wedding Banquet Garment** – Get Baptized - God **Loves You**. Amen.

51

Chapter 5 Covid-19 Dance

Whew!

You may not believe it but today is 3/30/2020 exactly one month since I transcribed the last chapter. And if you know History, you know we are in the midst of the COVID-19 Dance! As I call it.

Yes, the Coronavirus Epidemic now classified Pandemic has the whole world in its grip and almost everyone in *fear, anxiety* and *distress.*

But what has COVID-19 to do with 'Deep Cleansing'?

Every Nation on Earth:- Big or Small, Rich or Poor, First World or Third World; Religious or Not-Religious, Male Dominated or Female Liberated; Terrorist filled or Persecuted by the Holders of Power... Every Nation is in one form of *Isolation* or another. Yes, they are!

"Shelter in Place" the Leaders tell their Citizens, as they themselves scramble to distance themselves from the World!

If that was ever previously imaginable - as "flapping one's wings and inflating one's Ego; like the peacock"- had been the game-in-town for the 'Who- was- Who' of 2020.

And now;

Seems we have suddenly discovered Humility! COVID-19

has come to make every human being equal. How *Humiliating!* Professor Higgins in *"My Fair Lady"* would say.

"Shelter in Place!
Self- Isolate
Don't touch, Don't share
Wash your hands over and
over again
Spray and Disinfect
Your Environment"

And when you are Done
Just look at Yourself!

Alone with Yourself
Alone with Your Body
Alone with Your Mind
Alone with Your Spirit

Self- Isolate
Now you can find out-
Who you are
What you are
Why you are

When you are

What Interests You
What Annoys You
What Inspires You
What Saddens You

Now you want to know-
What is your Purpose
Why you are Here-

Might even be time to
contemplate-
Who have you helped in your
life
Who have you hurt in your life

What matters most to you
How will you be remembered
And most of all when you are
done:
Will your Spirit re-unite with
God
Or will it wander on
And on in melancholy-
Worse still will it

Go to the fiery furnace.

"No, this is not the time to snicker!" An old friend told me.

Deep Cleansing! Coronavirus, COVID-19 came to remind the World:-

The Big and the Mighty
The Small and the Weak
The Young and the Old
The Rich and the Poor
The Wise and the Foolish
All Humanity-
That we did
Not make Ourselves.

This visit was just a reminder from COVID-19 that Humanity did not create Humanity.

And in case we forgot or refuse to accept the reality; this tiny,

fragile, string of RNA-Virus
came to remind us-
"Man thou art dust, To dust
you must return,"
 [Genesis 3:19]
God created the World for
God. Obey the rules and live.
Disobey and die. The choice is
ours. That simple.

*****

So, before the COVID-19
Dance, were you in the *Fast
Lane* like most Humanity was:

Speeding off the Cliff with
Pleasures of the Flesh.
Over indulgent with Food,
Alcohol, Sex, Drugs and more.
Were you pursuing so much
Money and Power
You did not care the
Casualties
You left behind as you *Pleased*
Yourself and pursued

Your ambition

Little Girls may die
Or be Enslaved
For all you cared
You were just having Fun!

Or maybe
You were cheating and lying
for Profit
Creating alternate truths
When there is only One Truth
And then
You laughed it off
As "Smart"!

"That was great!" you said to yourself in *Covid-19 isolation.* Or did you think differently?

**Are you proud of who you are
and ready to meet God
The Ultimate Judge to hear:
"Well Done, Good and
Faithful Servant"
[Matthew 25:21]**

Or

"Depart from Me, you who practice lawlessness…"
[Matthew 7:23]

Oh Covid-19 Dance! Why do we have to *'Self Examine'*? It's too much pressure!

It makes us *anxious* and gives us *sleepless nights.* Let's change the *topic.*

Alas, we can't change the topic
We are in the middle of *Covid-19 Dance*
And we don't Control
The Beat!

So, are we now willing to *Humble Ourselves,* stop beating so pompously on our chests in pride and arrogance about *"How well we have*

59

conquered Nature" and obey the Rules of Nature laid down by God the Creator? Are we willing to plead for the Mercy of God and seek *His Wisdom* before it is too late for this Generation of Humanity?

Some say 'Yes'. Some say 'No'.

Oh, the Covid-19 Dance
The choices it presents-
Dance to the Left
Dance to the Right
Perhaps
Just stand still until the Dance
Is Over!

Or Is It?

*****

Chapter 6 Digging Deeper

Perhaps we want to dig even deeper about why we make all kinds of *excuses* for all the wrongs our Conscience tell us we are doing but blaming others for:

Are you blaming every fault
you find in Yourself
On your Mother
Your Father
Your Brother or Sister
Your Neighbor
Your Boss or Co-worker

Yes, "The Enemy has done it!"
No, it's "That One!"
From a different Ethnic Group
Language, Nationality, Tribe or
whatever:

For sure the blame is on
Your 'Political Enemies'
The 'Spoilers'

Maybe the issue is *Unforgiveness.*

You cannot forgive that Son of a …(something) or that … (something) of a Woman who offended you so badly years ago.

Yes, you know you are supposed to "forgive everyone who trespasses against you" as the Lord's Prayer requires but 'No, Not this one!' You will never forgive him or her; you resolve in yourself.

Then, again, this Covid-19 Dance might be a signal to replace *Unforgiveness* with *Forgiveness.*

It might make your Dancing Steps *lighter* and *surer*.

*****

Maybe you are not quite done. You might have one more level of cleansing that requires you *chastise yourself.*

What? Not look elsewhere? Why are we going back to these dead and archaic concepts that we buried long ago with our superstitious Forefathers? Covid-19 is only a virus. We will deal with it the way we have dealt with other viruses. Stop distracting and wasting my time!

Yes, indeed it is time to look *deeply inward* and *get mad, mad, mad as mad can be at yourself.* Because "You are the Man!"

Yes, "You are the Man!" that Person! The One Human, as Nathan, the Prophet told David the King; [2 Samuel 12:7] when David committed a series of sins and *ignoring* all his own sins, was quick to rise in *indignation* to condemn the *'wicked and oppressive'* man in Nathan's story. [2 Samuel 12: 1-13]

"So David's anger was greatly aroused against the man (in the story) and he said to Nathan, "As the Lord lives, the man who has done this shall surely die!

And he shall restore fourfold for the lamb, because he did this thing and because he had no pity." [2 Samuel 12:5-6]

Yes, *You* are the man, that Person in error -

Are you now ready to say
"The buck stops here"
I am responsible for My Life
And Decisions

Ready to say
I will now read *Psalm 51*
(David's Response)
With conviction and true
repentance?

If your answer is 'Yes' – That,
should give you Peace!

Chapter 7 **Compassion**

Covid-19 Dance over!
Maybe not forever, but at least it is taking a pause.

And while we recoup, we recall - Thankfully, that Our Father, God; Our Creator- is full of *Mercy* and *Compassion* for us His *stubborn* but *fragile* children.

We are reminded that He is the Father of the Prodigal Son, who squandered his *heritage* in *dissipation.* Living a wild and undisciplined life – until all was spent and nowhere to go!

He is the Father, who *so loved* His son, prodigal or not, that He was always on the look out for him to *return* home.

Did Covid-19 bring us to the end of our riotous living and are we ready to turn back and return to the Father's House?

The decision must be made individually but the message is that we must *first have a change of heart.*

A contrite heart willing to *change direction* and then **choose by your own 'free will' to turn back and *head* Home to the Father's House** where there is a *Banquet waiting for us (you and I!)*

Coronavirus, Covid-19 came to stripe Mankind of his *farceness* that he is invincible. He is a *genius with his Computer* and *Artificial Intelligence (AI).*

No! Man No! You can do nothing without God. And if, as in past

History records, you become too cocky and forget that 'dust you are'- and find it inconvenient to give God the *Glory due Him,* then a *fragile string of RNA virus* will come again to visit with *'A Dance'!*

"That's just Nature correcting itself," some wise crackers would say. Or, "That was a freak of Nature, don't worry about it!"

Centuries from now, Human descendants will consider the tale of Coronavirus Covid-19 **a story of their primitive forebearers in the 21st Century who could not figure out a simple RNA virus!** Imagine that!

To them, the Covid-19 Dance will sound like the story of the Israelites and the **Snakes that bit them to Death** as narrated in the Book of Numbers 21:4-9

It was reported that while the
Israelites were on a detour
Around Edom, on their way
from Egypt to their Promised
Land, they grumbled that they
had no water and the food
(Manna)
God gave them was
monotonous.
They were not grateful for
their *lives,* which
God had saved
So, God sent them 'fiery
serpents' [Numbers21:6]
Which bit many of them to
death.

"Therefore, the people came
to Moses and said,
"We have sinned for we have
spoken against the
Lord…" So Moses prayed for
the people. [Numbers21:7]
And a solution was given and
the people stopped dying

From epidemic snake bites!

Fairy Tale! Some may say.

It is worth noting that each Generation's Plague is proportional to their level of sophistication.

So, the migrating Israelites had Snakes to contend with and the modern High-tech Generation got Covid-19, a chastisement, consistent with their level of technology and lifestyle.

That said, the three points to note about the Serpent Chastisement are:

1. The Israelites had a change of heart and **acknowledged** there were in error. "We have sinned…" [Numbers 21:7]

2. They **named** their sin specifically, not generically.
   "… for we have **spoken** against the Lord and against you (Moses) [Numbers 21:7]

3. They **humbled** themselves and asked for Forgiveness and Mercy;
   "… Pray to the Lord that He take away the serpents from us" [Numbers 21:7]

"Moses prayed for the people," and guess what happened? God, the Loving Father, ever ready to Forgive His erring children responded favorably to them.

He instructed Moses to make a **Bronze Serpent** and put it on a pole raised high so that "… everyone who is bitten, when he looks at it, shall live." [Numbers 21:8]

Fairy Tale! Fairy Tale! Some may scream again; just as the future Generation of Humanity will call the Covid-19 Pandemic Dance a Fairy Tale by their **21st Century Ancestors**, who at its onset, had no idea how to deal with an Infectious RNA of a Virus, the way the Israelites did not know how to use *Anti-venom* against their biting snakes.

Yes, 'Fairy Tale, Fairy Tale', every Generation says; but God is the Same, Yesterday, Today and Forever. He will call His children to order when they become too cocky, fight too much among themselves or forget that they are ALL **Brothers and Sisters** - Children of One Father God, Almighty- who set us on Earth for His Glory.

73

Chapter 8 The Rich and The Poor

God, who set us on Earth for His Glory, did it as an *act of Love.* He is Our Father, but His True Name is **LOVE Eternal**

Because of His Eternal Love for us, He is present in our every **condition.** "He will never leave us or forsake us as he tells us through Joshua in Deuteronomy 31:8

"The Lord, He is the One who goes before you.
He will be with you,
He will not leave you nor forsake you;
Do not fear nor be dismayed."
[Deuteronomy 31:8]

So, Coronavirus Covid-19 was not there to destroy us but, as another voice, 'in the wilderness' crying out for us to *Pay Attention* to what we were doing to the Father's *garden* - Earth!

*****

When I started writing about **Deep Cleansing** on February 12, 2020; my human intellectual intention was to explore the *Physical Ailment* and the *Chronic Diseases* we suffer, because of *deep seated scars* we carry through from Childhood and other stages of life. They include the *Post Traumatic Stress Disorders (PTSD)* we don't even recognize many times!

At that time, I did not realize the **Whole World,** with **every Human Being** in it, was seriously ill! And if I had such an inkling, I would have dissuaded myself from **starting this book!**

But since it is not I, but the Holy Spirit who *Downloads* into my Brain, most of my writing, I transcribed the message which you have now read. And learnt as I went along also, that:

-*The Covid-19 Dance Experience was to Call the Whole World's Attention that-* **"All have sinned and fall short of the glory of God**…" [Romans 3:23]. The whole World was in need of repentance – turning back from its reckless *abuse* of the Earth

They said it was Chinese –
Wuhan ate a Bat
And birthed Coronavirus

But

The World is one –

Sunrise Sunset
Round and Round
It travelled - And every Nation
Coronavirus got.

The Strong could not *chase* it
away
Nor the Rich *buy* it off
So, the Jets and Planes
Private or Commercial
Grounded by Covid-19
Join the Dance!

When the Beat first begun-
The Poor thought
'Now, the Rich get to pay!' Ha
ha!
But the Poor was not Spared
Cos Covid-19 Dance is about
the Soul-
How poor is your Spirit- is
what counts
For "Blessed are the Poor in
Spirit"

[Matthew 5:3]

Then Hunger followed
The Dance- to intensify the
suffering
As it were
Where is God? - the Poor cry
To be hit twice as hard

The Cough will not stop
And Breathing with
Ventilators
The Poor do not have
So, with Empty Stomachs
They cry louder
"Is this Judgement Lord?"

"Not yet," they are told
***

But the Rich hung on longer
The 'Stock Market' and
'Money Markets'
Will soon rebound
And we shall get back to
Business as usual-
Oppress, Oppress, Oppress

Not our fault if the Poor
Keep looking up to God
Who we know does not exist
If God exists why will
Coronavirus come?
At this High Season of
Christian Lent in 2020
Let Him come down from the
Cross
And smash Coronavirus
And we will know He exits
For now, we shall keep on
Doing 'our thing!'

We know Our Money will save
us
We can count on that
It is safely locked away-
In the Bank Vaults,
Some of which are now Virtual
But it's still Our Money!

Chapter 9 Dancing On Sea and Land

The Covid-19 Dance did not take place only between the Rich and the Poor. The Sea and Land were also called to Dance!

Warring Nations Pause:

The Sailors are with
Coronavirus Sick
The Nuclear Sub-Marine Ships
To Stand-Still came

Anchor!
The Captains Command
So we can, the Covid-19
Dance!
Yes, the Russian Navy did the
Dance
As did the Dutch Navy

The British Royal Navy
will not be out danced
And definitely
Not the American All Powerful
Nuclear
Submarines who Covid-19
Danced
To perfection!

Meanwhile, on land, as each Nation 'sheltered in place' they peeped out of their Holes to remind each other who - had *more soldiers* and *fighting people*. And yes, who could annihilate the other, even the whole world, in a matter of seconds.

And the Beat went on...

II
Africa Came to Dance Too

And while the First nations danced on land and sea, some

Africans tried to snicker, but
were soon reminded:

You, African squirm
Remember
Your Leaders did not build you
Decent Hospitals
Even to Die in
In your Best Days

They, like you, are now
'Home-Bound' doing the
Covid-19 Dance
Sadly they learn 'Charity form
Home begins'
Cos the Mighty Nations
Will not them Visa grant
So they could add their
corrupt *Rhythm*
To their *pure* European and
American
Even Chinese
Covid-19 Dance

**By the way, No One Cursed
Africa**

**You reap what you sow
African Leaders
Have to begin to sow Good
So Africa can reap Good in the
Future
That simple.**

****

III

All Religions in Forms and Shapes Came to Dance!

We all know there is only *One Earth.* Even as we search the Universe of God's Creation for another earth! Never content with the One Truth that there is only One God, we push and shove at one another for our so called faith.

My Religion is better than yours
I am Hindu, Moslem, Christian

Jew I am
No! Confucian, Sikh, Tao
Call me Zoroastrian, Buddhist
Baha'i, Shinto
Jainism

Mine is the greatest
Our God is bigger than Yours
Ours the best religion
We will go to War, Fight, Kill
For Our Religion
Away with you Unbeliever-
You are dispensable
As far as our religion is
concerned
But
Why doesn't Covid-19 know
that

No, Covid-19 does not seem
to care
So every religion
Joined the Covid-19 Dance
Alas!

IV
Militants and
Fundamentalists also Danced

Militants and Fundamentalists of every ilk, pride themselves in their *purity of purpose.* So how dare the coronavirus make them do the *Common Dance*!

The Militants say
We are fundamentalists
We will not tolerate another
Color, Religion, Language or
Race

We have guns
And will shoot to death
Anyone who we do not like
We have stockpiled
ammunition
Ready for war ...
But Covid-19 Dance tune
Started playing
For us too!

Chapter 10 Then the Earth Cried

The Earth cried because Humanity did not see the *daytime blue skies* and the *ruddy warm colors* of Sunset –because they had covered the sky with smog and pollution from Los Angeles to Beijing.

The Earth cried because Pollution Index was just a number; people could care less about, as long as the Stock Market number was rising.

Yes, the Earth cried more because Wild Animal Depopulation had become alarming.
Human activity was causing their habitat degradation.

World Wildlife Fund, in lamentation at that time said:

"A delicate balance must exist among all

Living things in order to sustain healthy ecosystems.

Unfortunately, the balance has been thrown off By human involvement.

Mammal, bird, reptile, fish and amphibian populations have declined by 52% during the last four decades"
[worldatlas.com/articles/major-causes-of-decline-in-wildlife-populations-worldwide.html]
(Updated by Amber Parion August 14, 2018)
[Downloaded April 28, 2020]

Parion listed the seven major causes of wild animal depopulation as

1. Exploitation 37%,
2. Habitat Degradation/Change 31.4%
3. Habitat loss 13.4%
4. Climate Change 7.1%,
5. Invasive Species/Genes 5.1%
6. Pollution 4%
7. Disease 2 %

*****

II
Fire, Fire! Flooding Too!

As if to encore the wild animals' plight, the Fires came to burn and scorch the World.

California **burned** in endless Wild Fires; while the Amazon Forest **blazed** to hell, But Australia would not be outdone! The continent was encircled with **flames.**

According to the Center for Disaster Philanthropy, "As of February 15, 2020 more than 46 million acres (72,000 square miles) of land were burned in thousands of fires since June 2019. At least 80% of the Blue Mountains World Heritage area NSW and 53% of the Gondwana World Heritage Rainforest in Queensland (QLD) were burned …" [disasterphilanthropy.org 2019-australia-wildfire]

*****

And the Earth flooded. Maybe not as copiously as in Noah's Flood. But many nations suffered loss of lives and much distress

In Europe there were places in Austria, Hungary, Germany and Czech Republic that water covered the land for days. Italy's "Venice under Water" was the headline in 2019 for many weeks before Covid-19 became Italy's major dance, for a season.

Africa followed closely with its own flooding - Cameroon, Central African Republic, Ivory Coast, Ghana, Kenya and South Sudan, to name a few. And some unfortunate and abandoned people had to climb tree tops to stay alive, while the vultures hovered.

Southeast Asia led by the Philippines and Indonesia almost had all their islands drowned with the floods of August 2019. But Samoa and Burma (Myanmar), would not be out flooded so they too joined the flooding.

Then, Western India, Bangladesh and Pakistan closed the flooding loop for Asia as the Earth cried more.

For Brazil, in South America, heavy rainfall with previously unseen flooding and landslides that occurred in January 2020, devested the land, killed many people and displaced 30,000 - 45,500. Other South American nations with similar flooding issues included Paraguay, Peru, Ecuador and Bolivia. [F/N...]

III

And the Sea Raged

As the Earth cried, the **Sea Raged.** But not many Humans cared what happened to the **Sea**.

They continued with their parties and fun in the **Cruise Ships.** Sail Baby, Sail on! Who would want to stop?

Who cared that, according to Conservation.org; "Each year, we exposed the world's waterways to an increasing variety of pollutants – **plastic debris, chemical runoff, crude oil and more.**" [conservation.org/stories/ocean-pollution-11-facts-you-need-to-know] (Downloaded April 28, 2020).

These sources also said there are "more plastic than fish" in the ocean. What? Plastic in my belly? So, the Sea Raged!

*****

IV

Human Surprise

But Humanity appeared surprised, even initially irritated, that the insolent Coronavirus later known as COVID-19 dared to interrupt **Human Pleasure Circus** on this Earth which we call Our Home!

As part of *'Breaking News'*, [Wikipedia.org/wiki2020_corona virus_outbreak_in_cruise_ship] reported the following, at the time saying;

"British registered **Diamond Princess** was the first ship to have a major outbreak on board, with the ship quarantined at Yokohama from 4 February 2020 for approximately one month. Over 700 people became infected and 12 people died…"(Downloaded 4/28/2020)

Now, where did that come from! Humanity seemed stunned.

At this writing and as of 24 April 2020, over 30 cruise ships have had confirmed positive cases of coronavirus on board.

Never mind, as noted earlier that Navy Ships and Nuclear Submarines have also shared generously in the Covid-19 Dance.

And the Beat went on and still goes on and on.

*****

Chapter 11 Ears for Hearing and Eyes for Seeing

Ultimately, the Covid-19 message was for 'those who have ears to hear' [Mark 4:9] and 'those who have eyes to see' [Matthew13: 15-17]

It was, as it were, a brief moment in History for *Global Human Awakening!*

We know, we have the five major Senses of the body present in a **living** person – Eyes for seeing, Ears for hearing, Nose for smelling, Tongue for tasting and Skin for Feeling – but they are not fully functional in **sleep.** You have to be **awake** and possibly alert to optimize these five senses.

It seemed, however, that the majority of the Human Race, though not physically asleep, at that time, had gone from slumber to post orgasmic comatose in their reckless pursuit and gratification of Fleshly **Pleasure** – *Power, Money, Ego, Position…Excessive Eating, Drinking Alcohol, Getting High on Drugs and Substance, Sex, Human Trafficking, Stealing, Cheating, Lying, Killing other Human Beings and much more …*

In that human state of abandon – **"They had Eyes, but were not Seeing** what the **signs** of the time was telling them:

It was saying, STOP
Dismembering Mother Earth
She is being torn apart
Can't you See!

*****

Humanity had **Ears** as well, but were not **hearing** the 'Cry and Moan' of the Earth in 2020. No, the ears were not listening.

So what should be done to get the ears to hear?

Chapter 12 The Concept of Hearing

Sitting in a boat in water, while the people on dry land listened, Jesus the Teacher, explained the parable of the Sower which can be found in Mark 4:3-9.

Ah, the Wisdom for Our Time!

This parable of the sower, seems to hold the **key to Covid-19 dance!** But before we get there, let's check out the "The Concept of Hearing" in Human Life.

Hearing is about **Reception**, unlike seeing which is about Perception.

The sounds that hit the eardrums to activate the sense of hearing are just air waves.
Who receives the vibrations responds according to their **disposition.**

So, for example two people can hear the same music and respond totally differently. One may bob their head and tap their feet in relaxation and joy while **the other may be totally unmoved or even become melancholic because** the music reminded them of a loss of something.

In the interpretation of the parable of the sower, which followed the quote, "…and **hearing** they may hear, and not **understand**, lest at anytime they should be converted …" [Mark 4:12] Jesus, the Teacher, explained:

"And these are they by the
wayside, where the **word is
sown;**
But when they have heard,
Satan cometh immediately,
And taketh away the word
that was **sown in their hearts.**

These likewise are the ones
sown on stony ground who,
When they hear the word
immediately receive it with
gladness;
And they have no **root** in
themselves,
And so only endure for a time.
Afterward, when tribulation
arises for the **word's sake**
Immediately they stumble.

Now, these are the ones sown
among thorns;
They are the ones who hear
the **word,**
And the cares of this world,
The deceitfulness of riches,

And the desires for other
things
Entering in choke the **word,**
And it becomes unfruitful.

**But these are the ones sown
on good ground,**

Those who hear the word,
Accept it, and bear fruit:
Some thirtyfold, some sixty,
and some a hundred."
[Mark 4:14-20]

"If anyone has **ears to hear,
let him hear."**
[Mark 4:23]

It is obvious that **Hearing** is
dependent on Disposition –
the type of soil – wayside,
stone, thorn or fertile ground.

Which soil would you like? The
choice is yours.

Chapter 13 Choosing Well as Leaders

Leaders at every level of Society are the Bell Ringers for the Covid-19 Dance and for every other pandemic that will afflict mankind in the future, for that matter.

This is because *Leaders' Choices have Consequences on their Society. Leaders, at every level must, therefore, learn to 'Choose Well'.*

It was the choices made by Leaders, at all levels, that determined the consequences the People faced in the Covid-19 Dance! Yes. If your ears are listening and hearing –

\-   Let's start at the micro level, individual choices, and walk up the ladder to the Rich and Mighty choices:

Level 1: Individual Person

Me, myself and I
Decided, the Covid-19 Dance steps
To Avoid
'Cos the virus in **cold** thrives.
So I chose, in **warmth** of hot Tea
Coffee and Soup,
The virus to terminate.

**Level 2:
Parent and Head of Family**

The Covid-19 Dance
Our family will exclude,
Our Love and Health to protect.

So, to the Gym and
Playground
We will abstain,
Until Death no more tolls
At the gate.

Level 3:
Small Business/Corner Store

Owner
Covid-19 Dance, we know
The Breath can cease.
Grasping for Air
Oxygen tank cannot provide.
But
The Cash that us evade
We must try to grasp.

So, we hope the dance
Will be light
When we falter,
And only grieve
the ICU Respirator

Level 4:

Big Industrial Boss and CEO

Dance Covid-19, we dance
Dance O Dance
That we do all the time,
Changing partners too!
Let them die
Who must die, let them
They die, people die
That's what they do
Covid-19 Dance we must do -
Even enjoy
For who dies, will Tomorrow
Be replaced.

Level 5:
Town Councils/Local

Governments and Municipal
Leaders

We have this dance,
Many times before done.
Maybe called Covid-19 now
But it's the same tune
Same dance.

Social Activities –
Sports, Games, Drinks and Fun
Make our Society.
We swing like the hammock
chair
Hum like the Bee
Taxes must be collected
The people must work
Lest the 'good-life' to them
Expectation become!

Level 6:
The Governors

Different as different they
are–

"Save my people from the Evil
Dance!"
Some say.
While others say;
"Monkey could care!"
Let it rain

And let the flood carry who it
wants
The sun someday will shine
And the Beat goes on …

Level 7:
Presidents, Prime Ministers,
Heads of State

The Covid-19 Dance
Is great Instrument for Politics
Let them Dance
To the Left and to the Right
But never Stand Still
Because in the Middle
We don't know who
You will vote for.

Covid-19 the Dance of Power
Power - Leaders know how to
wield:
So
Let the Music Play
They say …

Level 8:
Kings and Queens

Kings and Queens – Anointed
by God's Chrism Oil
Do not, to anyone's music
dance -
So to Covid-19 Virus music,
they will not dance
Nor to Man's; Rock n Roll,
Yangko, Ballet, and Rhumba

"Be Still," they tell their
Subjects

"A quiet time, on your knees
With appeal to the Creator
Sore knees, may give you
But firm bodies
Will from you emerge
When Tomorrow comes"

**Yes, choosing well. The choices
we make are as varied as we are
many, but they are only "Well**

Chosen" when our "Conscience has Peace" with it.

"For what does it profit a man to gain the whole world and lose his soul." [Mark 8:36]

This is particularly applicable to **World Leaders** who for a season, think they are God, All Mighty and Powerful!

All Leaders should take note, because the decisions they make affect so many lives. Leaders should be particularly careful and prayerful when they make major decisions. Because:

"To whom much has been committed, of him they will ask the more." Luke 12:48]

There shall be much accounting for the decisions of All Leaders at every level on the last day.

"The servant who knows the master's will, And does not get ready Or does not do the master's will, Shall be beaten with many stripes."[Luke 12:47-48]

Chapter 14 Human Response

Then Humanity with all its Intellect, Knowledge and Wisdom got into the thick of the Dance:

Social Distancing
They called it -
Six feet you must stay
Or perhaps ten feet
Away from next Human
Lest the coronavirus skips a
beat and Jumps
Into your Throat or Nose
There to dwell
And make you
Dance, even faster

Distancing not enough
Cover your face
In Public,
At least half of it!

Leave your eyes open
Lest Blinded
You stumble and fall.
But Goggle them up
If you can.

Stay Home, they say
As the World with Cabin
Syndrome suffers
Loneliness, Depression and
Anxiety
Galore

Yet the music would not stop.
So, the World Danced and
Danced
Covid-19 to weariness -
Their Dancing Feet got tired
'When will the Dance-Master
Strike the last tune
And relief bring
To Humanity's weary feet?'
They asked with quivering
voices

The Body tired is getting -
As the Mind
With Fear and Anxiety
Overtaken
Leave Humanity Confused

Who shall they listen to?
Who shall they believe?
Who shall they follow his
advice?
Who knows the Covid-19
Dance?

Rhythm

Perhaps, it's time to turn
To the God many had denied.
To
The Creator
The One Who made Heaven
and Earth
Perhaps….

Chapter 15 Anyone There?

They say He is Merciful. Perhaps if the People cried out to Him for Help and Rescue as He did for the Israelites and their Serpent Scourge in the desert [Numbers 21:6-9], perhaps he will hear, and save Humanity once again.

Hope Kindled!
Maybe not so fast. Child of Man -Humanity! Did your Covid-19 message get you to turn back from your Human Recklessness?

This is called Repentance.
This means a change in the *Inner Being.* Turning away from old self to new self, being re-created.

Rules of Engagement

Everyone knows that *All Human to Human Relationship has a Contract, written or unwritten: Mother and Child, Husband and Wife, Teacher and Student, Buyer and Seller, … Yes, there are 'Rules for Engagement' for every aspect of Life.*

So, once rescued, are you willing to stop these negative attributes?

STOP

Cheating: Using false scales and measures to buy and sell products

Inflating prices and over profiteering

STOP

Lying: Bending the truth and giving excuses for the evil intent you know you have in your Heart

STOP

Killing: Physically, Mentally and Emotionally taking another

Person's Life and Reputation by eliminating them or making their lives 'Hell on earth.'
STOP
Oppressing: The Poor, Weak, Orphans and Powerless
STOP
Commercializing: Human Beings as spare parts to make Liver, Kidneys and other Organs for transplant and experimentation. Or just simply for sexual orgies
STOP
Insatiable Greediness: For Power, Position and Fame
STOP
Online Fraud: False and misleading news, information, advertising and Rumor Mongering
STOP
Your Political Correctness: Once you know it is a lie
STOP

Deceiving: Yourself and desist from whatever Your Heart, (Your Conscience) tells you is wrong
Will You STOP?
Mouthing: "We are All in this Together." But when you are given money or food to distribute among your neighbors in need; you keep large sums or quantities for Your Team, Family, Friends or Yourself alone!

*****

II

Choose Love

And once you STOP all these and whatever else your conscience tells you to stop, are you willing to **replace** them with more **Positive Attributes**

You may call these new choices, **"Self-Preservation,"** if you wish. The point is, now that you have been spared the scourge; is there a change of Heart with "Goodwill to All" in it?

Are you willing to **Accept:**
The concept that, "All men are created equal" as enshrined in the Constitution of USA

That all Human beings are Brothers and Sisters, Children of the same Father, God the Creator of Mankind

That God, the Father of Mankind is Holy and wants all His Children to be Holy like Him – because 'Holiness begets Holiness and does not un-holiness beget.'

*****

To be Holy, the **Rules of Engagement** are simple, requiring only two items:

>   1. First to Love God above all things [Luke 10:27]; Money, Power, Prestige

and all the Glamour of Physicality

2. Second, "Love your Neighbor as Yourself." [Luke 10:27]

Choose **Love** because Love never fails. It is the antithesis of all that led Humanity to the Covid-19 Dance -

"Love is patient, Love is kind.
It does not envy, it does not boast
It is not proud.
It does not dishonor others,
It is not self-seeking,
It is not easily angered,
It keeps no record of wrongs.

Love does not delight in evil
But rejoices with the truth.

It always protects,
Always trusts,
Always hopes

Always perseveres

Love never fails."
[1 Corinthians 13: 4-8]

Yes, Choose Love for Deep Cleansing so you can Live your Best Life!

Chapter 16 Yes, It Was War!

Some World Leaders in 2020, had said Covid-19 Pandemic was a **World War!** There were correct.

*Covid-19 was a War against Humanity
and Humanity Lost!*

Yes, the Coronavirus *'had come, had seen and had conquered'* with the Covid-19 Dance, which had challenged and humiliated Mankind.

It had humiliated Mankind at its ascribed **best** - in human arrogance and technology. And would have destroyed him -

But for Grace.

Yes, Grace and **Mercy** saved us. Otherwise, Historic Julius Caesar's - "terse report to the Roman Senate: *'Veni, Vidi, Vici'*" *(I came, I saw, I conquered)* would have been Covid-19's report to the '**Senate** of the **Universe!**' [www.yourdictionary.com>i-came-i-saw-i-conquered] (Referenced 5/13/2020)

How very tragic that would qhave been for Humanity.

*****

Yes, it is by Grace, that the Earth found a moment to take one 'Healing Breath' during this Dance because terrified Humans had gone into **hiding:**

The Shelter-in-Place **Pollution Index**
came down from **Crazy** to **Sanity** -
Yes, it did!

The worst number was 871 in
Macedonia in 2019
And today May 13, 2020 the
worst number is down to 549 in
Turkey

India whose number was 834
in 2019, is 156 today as I write,

Though the United Arab
Emirate (UAE) seems stuck on
348 in 2019 and 352
Even today.
Don't ask me why?

*****

Why Pollution Index helped Covid-19 Dance with Fury

To appreciate why Pollution Index helped the Covid-19 Dance do so much damage to Humanity, let's briefly review what the *World's Air Pollution Report of 2019* says about the

Health **Effects of Ambient Air Particles** on the general population.

It says that, "Worldwide ambient air pollution accounts for:

29% of all deaths and diseases from lung cancer
17% of all the deaths from acute lower respiratory infection
24% of all deaths from stroke
25% of all deaths from ischemic heart disease
43% of all deaths from chronic obstructive pulmonary disease

The measuring pollution index unit called PM2.5; "is defined as **ambient airborne particles measuring 2.5 microns in size.**" It is the main culprit in air pollution.

"Its microscopic size allows the particles **to enter the blood stream via the respiratory system** and travel throughout the body, causing far reaching health effects, including **asthma, lung cancer, and heart disease.**

Air pollution has also been associated with low birth weight, increased acute respiratory infections and stokes!"
[c:/user/omuch/Downloads/2019-World-Air-Report-V8-20200318,pdf]

If the above summary sounds **familiar,** it is because that is exactly what Covid-19 does. Starting from the respiratory system, it affects all the body system: stomach, liver, kidneys, joints, bones, blood vessels, heart, brain and everything else in between.

*****

Ostrich for Leaders

Still, Humanity, especially the Leaders, behaved like **Ostrich** when pollution of air or water was discussed.

They acted as if it was not their Planet – Earth that was the topic of interest. They 'ostrich-ed' on, even as the expanded report from the above source warned about Asia, as potential hot spot of **peril** for Humanity;

"Regionally, South Asia, Southeast Asia and the Western Asia, carry the highest burden of fine particulate matter (PM2.5) pollution overall, with only 6 of the 355 cities included meeting WHO annual targets in those areas. (That meant that 349 cities

of the 355 did not meet the set target.)

Collectively, Cities within these regions also rank highly in the 'top global city ranking' (for pollution). Pointing out that;

Of the World's top 30 most polluted cities during 2019, 21 are located in India. 27 in Southeast Asia, and all 30 cities are within Greater Asia." [F/N]

Any wonder Covid -19 started in Wuhan, Asia.

*****

III
Temporary Retreat

Decreased Combustion

Fought to a standstill, Humanity was temporarily forced by Covid-19 to curtail some of its pollution activities by making less airborne particles from **vehicle engines combustion, industrial activities, fires and coal burning for energy production and other uses.**

Decreased Oil Prospecting

The Oil and Gas industries slowed down too! So much did, frightened Humanity, "shelter-in-place" that by mid-April 2020 World Oil prices had fallen to the floor; even below it –

"US Crude oil price go NEGATIVE AS DEMAND DISAPPEARS," NPR flashed on April 20, 2020.

"The key US oil benchmark, West Texas Intermediate settled at negative $37.63 ... So some traders, instead of paying to **buy** oil, were ready to pay as much as

$37.63 to get someone to **accept delivery** of one barrel of oil.

The coronavirus pandemic has led the global economy to slam the brakes, leading to an extremely sharp drop in demand for oil. It has created a massive oil glut and raised concerns about the lack of physical storage space for it."
[npr.org/sections/coronavirus-live-updates/2020/04/20/838521862/free-falling-oil-prices-keep-diving-as-demand-disappears]

Earth Takes a Break

Unimaginable!

But the measurable decrease in air and water pollution and in **oil and minerals prospecting - digging, drilling, fracking** and other activities, - gave *the Earth a moment to take a 'Deep Breath' of temporary Relief!*

So, the Earth stopped Crying for a brief while: No new Wild Fires, No major Earthquakes, No Tsunamis, No Typhoons, No big Volcanic Eruptions and No major Sandstorms. It was;

"Peace be Still"
If only for one Breath!

*****

Wild Life returns too!

Earth's Wild Life, upon seeing mother Earth take a breath, seemed to say, **"my turn please."**

Several YouTube videos featured wild Animals in every continent making some statement like, **"Hey, you Humans, we are still here. Remember us?"**

One such video titled *"Animals Take Over the Streets As Humans Stay Indoor Amid Lockdown"* elaborated the experience thus;

"While human beings are confined to their homes Due to the coronavirus-related lockdown across India, animals such as peacocks, elephants and even Nilgai (antelope), were spotted freely roaming city streets"
[Yardhype.com]

In the same vain *Inside Edition,* reported- "WILD PIGS IN PARIS STREETS."

It also reports that;

"The animals seem to be exploring places that they did not get to while humans roamed the streets. Pigs, Goats, Monkeys,

Rats and more animals take over the streets as humans go under extensive quarantine amid COVID-19 outbreak."
[Inside Edition ….] [F/N..]

Yes, Humanity lost the War but for Grace and Mercy go you and I.

Chapter 17 Before the Music Started

America I am
America I am
Rich and Powerful I am
Don't care if NATO lives.

WHO, UNICEF, and IMF
May to Blazes go

America I am
Power and Influence I have
To Sanction the Nations, I can't stand
If I want, when I want
And how I want it.

Who can stop me
So, to you, daring Leaders, I say
Remember   my   **Nuclear Buttons**

Are bigger than yours
And I can push them at will

Yes, America I am
Care   nothing   about
Environment
Pollution will go by itself
Capitalist I am
And only **money** speaks to me

And then;
The Covid-19 Bell rings…

II. European Union
European Union we are
And united we **cheat and steal**
From All Nations, not in Europe

For African Leaders and Latin
American cohorts,
We keep their stolen monies
Which in futility, they hope to
collect later-
Much, much later they wait

As surely, we know
These monies are now
Ours to keep

Fruit of our colonization!
See Africa today - still paying
Taxes to us
For in Ignorance and with
Language barrier
We made their Ancestors
Bequeath us
All their wealth-
Until we empty every ounce
O Gold and Diamond in Africa's
Belly
Yes!

European Union Strong we are
About to drown all those
Menacing Immigrants in the
Sea
Then,
 We hear the Covid-19 Bell ring

...

What's that?

III Middle East, Center of the World

Middle East we are
'Cos no one can us Name
For before History
We, here, have been

Dry and Hot in Places
Never mind,
For Our Bowel filled with
The Black Jewel of industry –
Oil
Oil and more Oil
We have no cares

With Oil Money
We can buy what we will
Even offer to pay for
Proud Americans to send
Their Sons and Daughters
As Soldiers to fight our
enemies
And buy their Boeing 737 or
Whatever

For Cash, if they prefer
While we self-indulge

And
For the World's Naïve
We offer Pilgrimages
As spiritual obligations

And as they trod in
Like herds of cattle
Their silver, gold, diamond
And more precious jewel they drop
In our Hotels and Shrines
Refilling our inexhaustible wealth

Oh the Smarts!

Their Women may come and go But ours, robed and covered in modesty
Can barely see through their eye-slit And who cares to see, for adorn and

Laden with gold, diamond and
precious gems
They barely move -
So in luxury and contentment
They indulge

Yes, we also sponsor wars
In nearby nations
To stay entertained
And let them remember
We have more Money than
them all

Then the Bell rings...
What's that?

IV Africa Says

I am Africa and I have
perfected the Art of
Crying;   Exploitation,
Oppression
Colonization
While we rob, kill and maim
Each other

The Leaders use
Tribe, Language, Religion and
whatever
To justify their
Thievery
Selfishness
Lack of Self and Community
Care

First we blamed
Britain, France, Germany and
Portugal
Even Belgium
The Italians did not make the
initial cut
So, now it is
The Indians and Chinese we
blame
For Africa Retard

Yes,
We kill other Africans
We take their lands
Force them out of their
Rich lands

Use cattle and sheep to
destroy their crops
And drive them out of the land

We pay Mercenaries,
Hire uneducated, hungry
Boys as foot soldiers
Arm them with AK- 45
And grant them "License to
Kill"
And maim

Rape as much as they wish
Just don't come back to tell the
Boss you ran out of money
'Cos he is busy
Living the Goodlife
While other Africans suffer
And die

Not his concern
No schools, No Hospitals
No safe place in Africa
For refuge -
Neither Churches nor Mosques
Can shelter you

I am Africa
Leaders and Followers alike
Take No Responsibility for
anything:
Not for Africa's life
As long as the White or Yellow
man Can be blamed

They call me
Africa Retard!

And then the BellRang….

V Asia We Are

We are Asia, Don't mess with
us
We are large and vast
We can do anything we want

We invent and make
All the World's desirables -
Cars, Boats, Airplanes
Clothing and Fancy Furniture
too

Food,   Drinks   and
Pharmaceuticals
If you happen to be sick

Don't forget your Computers,
Cell Phones, T.V and Music
Players
We make them also

Is there anything the World
needs That Asia does not make

Yes, sometimes Hong Kong,
Bangladesh,
North   Korea   and   the
Philippines
Dance off beat
But that's only for a season

We make Pollution
So thick – we cannot see the
Sky
Right above us

We are Asia

We move fast, very fast
So yesterday, today and
Tomorrow become One Day

We are Magic Masters
And set -
To dominate the World.
America may scream and
shout
We make everything it uses
It cannot do without us
So, who cares
If America shouts -

We are Asia
We can make anything we
want
Any time we want

And Covid-19, though not by
us made
First came from us

And then
The Bell rang ...

144

Chapter 18 "To Your Tents Oh Humanity!"

The Bell Rang and it said, *"Scamper- 'To Your Tents Oh Humanity!'"* echoing, as it were, the story of how King Rehoboam, the son of Solomon lost Ten of the Twelve Tribes of Israel to Jeroboam the son of Nebat, as he returned from self-exile in Egypt, where he had fled to escape King Solomon's wrath.

This account is given in both 1 Kings 16:1-17 and 2 Chronicles 10:1-16 and is worth reading because it distinctly shows the difference in World View of **Elders with life-experience versus impetuous Youth** thirsting for action without contemplating **consequences.**

Jeroboam lost Ten of the Twelve Tribes of Israel because he would not *choose goodness and kindness over arrogance and roughness.*

Believe it or not the issue was **Taxes!** *"Your father (Solomon) made our yoke heavy, but you make it lighter on us"* [2 Chronicles:10-10] *and we will serve you."* The people of Israel had requested of King Jeroboam.

The Elders advise to Jeroboam, was; *"If you are kind to these people and please them, and speak good words to them, they will be your servants forever"* [2 Chronicles 10:7] but the young King Jeroboam rejected this advice in favor of the Youth advice.

Saying, *"My little finger shall be thicker than my father's waist!*

And now, whereas my father put a heavy yoke on you, I will add to your yoke; my father chastised you with whips, but I will chastise you with 'scourges!'" [2 Chronicles 10:10-11]

Jeroboam may have scored a point for the Youth, Hi-Fifing each other and possibly Chest-to-chest bumping, but it was only for a blink of the eye because:

Now follows the consequence of wrong choice –

"Now when all Israel saw that the king did not listen to them, the people answered the king saying:

"What share have we in David? We have no inheritance in the son of Jesse.

Every man to your tents, O Israel!
Now see to your own house, O David!"

So, all Israel departed to their tents." [2 Chronicles 10:16]

And the Twelve Tribes have never become one nation since then.

Yes, **Choices have consequences**. We already discussed why all choices be it by individuals, families, communities, corporate entities, leadership at every level - Presidents, Prime Ministers, Kings or Queens matter. [Chapter...]

*****

In the year 2020, though it is not ancient Israel crying out to Jeroboam, the message is the same; **'To Your Tents Oh Humanity!' Look after your own survival, and don't wait for others; leadership or government to save you from the yoke of slavery to materialism and sin.**

There are lethal consequences for bad choices!

Covid-19 simply came as a 'Bell-Ringer', the 'Wake-up' Alarm for 21st Century high-tech Generation who do not believe in the concept of sin or that choices have significant consequences. Yes, it came, not to destroy but to alert the Generation that believes everything is due to Chance! - That there is a Creator behind every Universal occurrence.

The Bell first rang in China. A city called Wuhan was caught up in the initial Dance of Death, Death and more Death!

And the people scrambled with a *thousand (1000) bed Tent Hospital* built in 2 weeks to no avail. Dead bodies piled till there was no more room for storage. Cremation became the order of the day, as thick unbreathable air also became the reality for survivors in the city. So 'to their tents' for life's breath, they went into nooks and crannies to escape the scourging *coronavirus.*

Then The World Dance Began

As the World baffled over Wuhan, the Princess Cruise initially sailing in abandon found they had *'a visitor accompanying'* them. And the Covid-19 Dance started

*Keep them all at sea, some
said
Quarantine it was called
So they sailed round and
round
No place to anchor-
And
When in anchor they came,
Were told
'Your Human cargo
Dancing Covid-19
Cannot be unloaded'
So
Like Noah in the Ark
They were told to
Stay on Board.
But with Time
The Dance seemed to slow
A Break, perhaps for
Some to disembark.*

Meanwhile, the baton was
passed on to Italy –
*And it was
Death for Breakfast
Lunch and Dinner*

Death for Days on end

But Spain will not be left behind,
so it joined

And the United Kingdom

> *To outdo Europe*
> *Had Prime Minister*
> *Boris Johnson*
> *Dance into British*
> *ICU (intensive care unit)*
> *The Sound of Covid-19 Music*
> *To share!*

Still America will not be outdone
–

> *So New York*
> *The Empire State*
> *Danced, and Danced*
> *And Danced*
> *Almost took*
> *The breath of America*
> *Away!*

Then All the Nations cried out –

Mercy Lord!
Please save us
Remember We Are
The only Humanity
You got
"Or Don't You Care that
We Perish?"
[Mark 4:38]

Then Jesus said, "**Peace be Still.**" [Mark 4:39]

It seemed, for a moment, like a **new day** is dawning for mankind as Covid-19 Dance slowed to a whimper and may even become "still" like the sea.

Or was that my imagination...

Will there be another Storm?
If so,
How ready will the World be?

Chapter 19 A New Beginning

Like Noah's Ark, which many consider fiction or allegory, because in their head and imagination "No rain can fall so much to **drown** this Earth!"

In the same vain, "No insect, no ant, let alone a weak, single stranded RNA of a virus can cover the Earth and send all the Super Powers of the World scrambling into their hole!" Shelter-in-place they called it.

The Rich hunkered in their Estates, Mansions, Luxury apartments, houses and more.

Others in their Historic architecture homes, modern slums and ancestral huts.

While the Homeless and Disenfranchised, stayed put; in their cardboard homes, under the bridges, canopies and tree homes.

It did not matter what category of Human You were, You Hunkered down somewhere- *"waiting for the 'plague' to pass you by!"*

Then, in a form of repentance, as if we cared to 'mend' our ways **Governments;** with China leading, started to **Clean and Disinfect everything: Seen and Unseen!**

It was China that first donned itself – *Suited in complete Battle Gear-*

In full Star-War regalia,
From Head to Feet covered
And with

Latest technology enabled,
From trucks and Spray Mobiles –

Spewing Copious Chemicals and
Disinfectants.
Then they sprayed and hosed
down everything in sight
Homes, Shops, Markets and
Streets
Public Transportation Vehicles
Public Buildings, Offices, Parks,
Lots and more

Then Europe followed suit,
Washing, Cleaning, and Polishing
And hosing down every nook
and corner Of the continent
And when New York
Entered the Cleansing Exercise,
It would not be outdone
Sports Arenas, Stadiums
Beaches and Pools
Were not forgotten.
However, Africa
Who lacked bathing water in
Good-Days,

For Covid-19 found- No Water
For Cleansing!
And
Pathetic Nigeria,
Africa's largest Nation, in
Population
Whose Leaders and Cronies
Drilled and siphoned the
Nation's Oil
To reckless abandon
Leaving devastating ruin and oil
spillage behind.
Yes, Africa's Giant, indeed
Had Oil Pipelines everywhere
For Leadership thievery -
But
No Running Water pipes or taps
To wash and spray their streets
Of endemic Squalor
So
They died and died
Kano City said it was
"A Strange Disease"
Suddenly killing their people
But "it was not Covid-19!"
Why?

Because the people were not
tested
They said.

Then
Coming later to the Dance
Latin America
Had its own Madness
So Brazil
Danced with the Giant
Wreckers
America and Russia
And
President Jair Bolsonaro
Enchanted by the Music
And averse to Cleansing
Asked, "So What?" Covid-19
"What do you want me to
do?"
Nothing, Sir
Nothing! We said.

Chapter 20 Life Lessons from Covid-19 Dance

1. Rethinking Destructive Technologies:

Part of the choices to make about deep cleansing our planet must include *rethinking and redesigning the planet's destructive technologies.*

For example, Petroleum Engineers and Technicians should go back to the drawing board, in view of the Covid-19 experience and anticipated future Pandemics, if Humanity does **not change its behavior and attitude to our planet, Earth.**

Their focus should not be mainly on **how much monetary profit** they hope to get but also on **sustainable mutually beneficial processes for Man and Planet** to co-exist.

It is true that Modern Man depends heavily on the Petroleum and Gas Industries for countless products like: -

Gasoline, Jet fuel, Kerosene, Plastics, Tires, Ink and Paint. Roofing shingles, Asphalt, Bug Killers and Wax Paper. Plus Vaseline, Shoe Polish, Nylons, Cosmetics, Candles, Sealing wax, Novelty Candy, Crayons, Paper cups and more...
[Earth Source Week, Products made from Petroleum. www.earthsciweek.org/classroom-activities/products-made-petroleum] Downloaded 05/26/2020

And there is no doubt that these Products, enhance the Quality of Life for Mankind but there must be a balance between good and harm.

Using our collective **Human Intellectual Asset**, we must find this **balance.**

Petroleum products like **plastics** should not be so ubiquitously 'that there are more plastic in the Ocean than fish!' as we noted earlier in this presentation. [Chapter...]

The Guardian April 05, 2017 report says; "The disposal of plastic bottles is a global issue. Every year millions of single-use bottles end up in landfill sites or in the ocean and very small proportion are recycled. ..." [www.theguardian.com/environment/201 7/apr/05/how...] Downloaded 05/26/2020

Drilling down further on this problem, it reports on June 28, of the same year 2017 that;

"More than 480bn plastic drinking bottles were sold in 2016 across the world, up from 300bn a decade ago. If placed end to end they would extend more than half way to the Sun. By 2021 this will increase to 583.3bn according to most up to date estimate from Euromonitor International's global packaging trend report." [theguardian.com/environment/2017/jun/28/a-minute-worlds-plastic-bottle-binge-as-dangerous-as-climate-change] Downloaded 05/26/2020

*****

Without, further ado, you can see that the problem was identified and alarm sounded, at least in 2017, but it took until 2020 with the Covid-19 Dance for all

Humanity to get the gist that beyond technology, individual choices matter to the *health of our Planet and People.* Next question is are we willing to re-think our *personal choices for common good?*

1. Rethinking Personal Choices for Common Good

Yes, our current cultural attitude of **Me, Myself and I are the only Ones that matter,** does not seem to include 'Common Good' as participant in our daily life.

Unfortunately, this was the fruit of people coming out of - *serial oppression-* as well recorded throughout the History of Mankind.

Self-assertion, *'I am somebody and I matter,'* which was intended to help each person grow into **their own fullness of personhood**, swung the pendulum too far to the other side.

Self - Entitlement, became the order of the day, whether we worked for it or not: *"It's mine and I want it Now! No, I can't Wait! Why should I wait?"*

And when it comes to taking responsibility for anything, minor or major; *"Don't look at me, It's not my fault. So and So did it! They are responsible, not me!"*

And after reading the above section on **Technologies**, we feel even better blaming Corporate Entities instead of ourselves for the precarious state of planet Earth. *"Sure,"* we say, *"See Corporate Greed! See how much profit they make polluting and dismembering the Earth without* *a care. Yes, let's sue them for* **compensation!** *And then let's do more* **shopping** *with the pittance we receive!"*

Yeah!

Yeah indeed, but it is our **Personal Life-Style choices** that fuel the **corporate entities activities.**

Most of the products from Petroleum and Gas Industries listed earlier; like Cosmetics, Shoe polish, Paper cups and one-time-use-plastic containers for drinks and more are produced to **satisfy our personal life style demands!**

The referenced *Guardian* report puts it like this:

"The demand, equivalent to about 20,000 bottles being,

bought every second, is driven by an apparently insatiable desire for bottled water and the spread of a western, urbanized "on the go" culture to China and the Asia pacific region." [theguardian.com/environmental/2017/jun/28/a-minute-worlds-plastic-bottle-binge-as-dangerous-as-climate-change]

So, we are back to *'You Are the Man! That Person, That Human Being'* contributing to both the Corporate Greed and our Environmental Degradation!

Doesn't feel right. No, it doesn't.

Time to re-think our personal choices for common good. Every little effort helps. Can you do that?

*****

2. Rethinking Leadership Responsibilities for Human Survival

Before the Covid-19 dance, Leadership at every level was about Ego and is still so even now.

*"I am your leader because I
was elected Chairman
Of Counsel
I am charming and great!
I can be anything you want me
to be for you
As long as you bow and
tremble
In my presence.*

*Sure, I cheat and lie from time
to time
Who doesn't do that?
It is the Art of the Con-
Business Trade of Leadership
Unless you prefer the heavier
type with
Threats and Arm-twisting*

*Even Arm-breaking if
necessary*

*With my name and face
Donning every news media
Making it clear
I am the chosen leader
I love my Power and Influence
A lot
And will not give them up
For all the Gold in Fort Knox
And you only have to try to
run against me
To know where I am coming
from -*

*I am Chairman!
That's What I Mean.
Got it?"*

■ ■

Humanity's innate self-centeredness, manifested and magnified by Leaders, throughout the World, in their grandiosity - create a situation where Every Society is a Reflection of the Leadership it has.

Peaceful Society: Tend to have calm, cool headed, fair minded and peace-loving leaders encouraging harmonious living.

Restless and Agitated Society: Tend to be led by Conniving oppressors who are even more self-centered and expediency propelled.

Progressive Society: Tend to have Thoughtful and Community oriented leaders; seeking "Common Good."

Retarded Unprogressive Society: Tend to have Self-absorbed, short sighted, retarded leaders who delude themselves they are 'progressive' while they can hardly think beyond the next meal.

Which Society is yours and who are your leaders at every level?

When you choose your leaders by consent, force or expedience you create the Society you live in.

Yes, Leaders can be impositional; but they do not usually last long without the consent or connivance of most of the people they lead.

Society is not hopeless. Autocratic, Democratic, Communist, Military or even Monarchy; "The Majority always Rules," because, no Human Being born by a Woman on this Earth can suppress Freedom without the help of other Human Oppression Enablers.

And while we are on the issue of Human Motherhood, Mothers **should take note and raise their children with the idea of 'Good Leadership' in mind.** Just in case!

[insert "Special Life Lessons from COVID-19 for the Fearless"]

These 'Key Highlights' are inserted between Chapter 20 and the concluding Chapter 21 because they contain additional insight into the subject of this book. These insights could make much difference to Truth Seekers. You never know.

It could be the difference between Life and Death, here on Earth or life and death, even after our first death; which is called Second Death, which God Forbid, no one should aspire to.

In inserting this segment, I note that being 'Politically Correct' is not an option for me because there is only One Truth.

Here are some key points dancing in my head:

1. *Jesus is Truth, Light and Life but Sin thrives in Lies, basks in secrecy and like Covid-19 hates light so cannot stand exposure to the light of truth.*
2. *Love is Life, Joy and Laughter but Sin is Death, Sadness and Depression*
3. *Jesus is Love and Togetherness in Unity but Sin Hates and Divides the People, pulling them apart from God and from each other.*
4. *Activities that bring Joy, Happiness, Brotherliness like Sports and Games, make the World Happy; while Human activities that*

Pollute or make Covid-19 thrive destroy the Wellness, Beauty and Fullness of Earth.

5. *Covid-19 Isolates, leads to loneliness and Bad outcome like sin does ultimately causing despair and death, sometimes violent; like suicide and gunshots*

6. *Humanity's initial solution of "shelter-in-place" appeared helpful at first, but was unstainable because Human Beings are inclined to be communal, not in separate cages*

7. *Humanity ultimately learned to live in conscious awareness of potential Covid-19 but kept it at bay by avoidance, sanitizing the environment and possibly sterilizing it with UV light*

8. *Just as with Sin, we learn to live with its potential injury, but keep it at bay by avoidance – Sanitizing through Prayer and destruction by exposing it to the Light of Christ Amen*

****

If you choose well, you will bear much good fruit, that is, more people who see you will want to be like you in goodness, mercy and all the virtues of the Holy Spirit.

The coronavirus bore much fruit too, except it was evil fruit with death as harvest. At the beginning of the Pandemic we were told 1 person infected up to 2-4 people which expanded in geometric proportion to encompass the whole world.

In a similar fashion, if you choose well and influence 2-4 people by lighting up their lives, your light of good choices will spread all over the world in the same geometric fashion, as long as you pass on the torch. Choose well.

*****

Those who believe and trust in the Mercy of God, Our Father will get to the Universal Promised Land which is Heaven, Abode of The King Forever – Amen!

Chapter 21 Model Leadership and Hope for Humanity

Jokes aside, some Leaders, brag about how clever and invincible they are because they can **Lie and Deceive** their Community, Region, Zone, State, Nation, Continent or even the whole World with endless fabrications.

In fact, some have become so proficient they even believe their own lies!

Unfortunately for them **'a lie is a lie is a lie'** and it can only come from a source we spoke about at the beginning of this book and clearly identified in John 8:44

"You belong to your father, the devil, and you want to carry out

your father's desires. He was a murderer from the beginning, not holding to truth, for there is no truth in him.
When he lies, he speaks his native language, for he is a liar and the father of lies."
[Bible Gateway-: father of lies www.biblegateway.com/quicksearch/?qui cksearch- ...]

In case you do not recall why he got the *'father of lies'* title, here is the explanation:

"So, Satan is not only the 'father of lies,' but of all those who suppress the truth. From the beginning, Satan has been a liar. He told his first lies to Eve, to deceive her and draw her away from God. (Genesis 3: 1,4)
He was the first liar which makes him "the father of lies" in the same way that Hippocrates is the *father of modern medicine."*

[www.compellingtruth.org/fat
her-of-lies.html]

Lying Leaders who think they are appointed by God, better think again, because **"by their fruit, you shall know them"** [Matthew 7:16].

By bearing lies for fruit, they let the World know who their 'father' is!

*****

Of course, there is always **Repentance** if they so choose.

*****

Good Leaders and Aspiring Good Leaders, inclined toward accomplishing the right and truthful leadership responsibilities need a Model to focus on.

The characteristics of such a model based on 'Common Good' require that such leaders;

1. Keep their Community Safe
2. Maintain Peace and Good Neighborliness
3. Provide appropriate Sustenance; Food, water, sanitation and basic necessities
4. Even provide occasional community Banquets and Festivities to lighten the people's heart and put a smile on their faces
5. Help make them more Contented because they are 'not in desperate want!'
6. And encourage the Spirit of Friendship and Goodwill to one another

These expectations are what every Human being deeply desires in their Heart from their Leadership. And the Psalmist in

Psalm 23 articulates it profoundly, for us –

The Lord is my shepherd; I shall not want.
He maketh me to lie down in green pastures: he leadeth me beside the still waters.
He restoreth my soul: he leadeth me in the paths of righteousness for his name's sake.
Yea, though I walk through the valley of the shadow of death, I will fear no evil: for thou art with me; thy rod and thy staff they comfort me.
Thou preparest a table before me in the presence of mine enemies: thou anointest my head with oil; my cup runneth over.
Surely goodness and mercy shall follow me all the days of my life: and I will dwell in the house of the LORD forever.
[KJV Psalm 23: 1-6]

And **Humanity's Good Shepherd**, the **Ideal Leader,** identifies himself in John 10: 11-18, saying, *"I am the good shepherd. The good shepherd gives his life for the sheep….. And I lay down My life for the sheep."* (John 10: 11, 15)

While no one is asking any Leader to lay down their life for their followers and community; the above quote, clearly **shows the shepherd's commitment to the flock's welfare.**

To make this point stick, Jesus gave us Peter, as model Community Leader, a Shepherd for the Followers. To succeed in this position, he must **love** first and then tend and feed the sheep and lambs.

"…Jesus said to Simon Peter,
"Simon, son of Jonah,

Do you love Me more than these?" ...
"...Feed My lambs."
"...Tend (Take Care of) My sheep."
"...Feed My sheep."
[John 21: 15-17]

It was only after this **Leadership Training** that Jesus said to Peter, *"Follow Me."* [John 21:19]. Not just as a Disciple but as **'A Leader, A Shepherd'** of the people.

We should take note.

*****

Perhaps, as Humanity undergoes this **Season of Deep Cleansing**, Leadership should *remold itself* in the example of Peter and in the **nature of the Good Shepherd**.

First, love the people under your charge. If you cannot, maybe you should seek another job or responsibility. Because it is only with love first, that you can find the fortitude to 'tend and care' for people.

*****

Finally, **Community itself**, should consider remolding the pervasive selfishness and mediocrity of future leadership by **requiring "Leadership Training Program for ALL Elected Leaders"** before they resume their chairs.

Universities all over the world, should look at this option for the **"Common Good of Humanity."**

Thanks for your Time and for Caring to read this.

Bibliography

- *The Lancet:* thelancet.com/journals/lancet/article/PIISO140-6736(20)31095-3/fulltext Downloaded 05/25/2020
- *The Telegraph* [Harriet Alexander, The Telegraph, May 17, 2020] Downloaded 05/21/2020
- The Holy Bible, New King James Version (NKJV), Thomas Nelson Bibles, Thomas Nelson Inc. USA 1994 www.ThomasNelson.com
- Chizea, Dora Obi. *The Problem with Pleasure*

www.ingramcontent.com/pod-product-compliance
Lightning Source LLC
Chambersburg PA
CBHW051451050726
47593CB00005B/2018